WHAT IF GOD TREATED YOU, THE WAY YOU TREATED ME?

Finding Freedom in Forgiveness

CHELETA BUDDO-GAYLE

WHAT IF GOD TREATED YOU, THE WAY YOU TREATED ME? Copyright © 2024. Cheleta Buddo-Gayle. All Rights Reserved.

Printed in the United States of America.

No portion of this book may be reproduced, stored in a retrieval system, or transmitted in any form or by any means, except for brief quotations in printed reviews, without the prior written permission of DayeLight Publishers or Cheleta Buddo-Gayle.

ISBN: 978-1-958443-74-3 (paperback)
978-1-958443-77-4 (hardback)

Scripture quotations marked (NIV) are taken from the Holy Bible, New International Version®, NIV®. Copyright © 1973, 1978, 1984 by Biblica, Inc.™ Used by permission of Zondervan. All rights reserved worldwide.

Scripture quotations marked "ESV" are from the ESV Bible® (The Holy Bible, English Standard Version®), copyright © 2001 by Crossway Bibles, a publishing ministry of Good News Publishers. Used by permission. All rights reserved.

This book belongs to:

_____

DEDICATION

To every heart that has ever struggled with the weight of unforgiveness—towards yourself or others. May this book be a gentle whisper from God's loving heart to yours.

May the words in this book inspire you to release the burdens of resentment and bitterness, and to embrace the liberating power of forgiveness. May you experience the transformative love and grace of God, and may you be empowered to share that love with a world in need. May this book be a source of comfort, encouragement, and liberation as you navigate the challenges of relationships and friendships.

To the women who feel trapped in cycles of resentment and hurt, may you find the strength to break free and embrace the beauty of forgiveness.

To the married couples who struggle to love and accept each other's imperfections, may you discover the transformative power of grace and mercy in your relationship. And to anyone who has ever felt the weight of unforgiveness, may this book be a reminder that you are not alone, and that God's mercy and love are always within reach.

May you find freedom in forgiveness, and may you discover the joy and peace that comes from living a life that reflects the heart of God.

With love and prayers for your journey,
Cheleta.

ACKNOWLEDGMENTS

I am truly grateful to have reached this milestone—the publication of my first book! It has been a dream come true, and I am thankful for the opportunity to share my words with others.

To God, my ultimate Source of inspiration and strength, I offer my deepest gratitude. May this book be a testament to Your love, grace, and mercy, and may it bring hope and encouragement to all who read it.

As I reflect on the journey of writing this book, I am filled with gratitude for the people who have supported me along the way.

To my husband, Christopher, your love and encouragement has been a constant source of strength.

To my family, your unwavering belief in me have meant the world. Thank you for being my cheerleaders.

To my friends, your prayers, contributions, and feedback have enriched this book in ways I could never have imagined.

To my editors, your proficiency and keen eye for detail have been invaluable. Thank you for helping me shape this book into its final form.

To DayeLight Publishers, your dedication, expertise and

passion have been instrumental in bringing this project to life.

To my dear readers, thank you for joining me on this journey. Your support means the world to me.

Thank you to everyone who has played a part in this journey. Your love and encouragement have made this book possible.

TABLE OF CONTENTS

Dedication vii
Acknowledgments ix
Introduction 17
What If God Treated You, The Way You Treated Me? 20
Forgiveness, Grace and Mercy 22
Forgiveness is a Choice 25
Part 1: "The Shattered Melody" 31
    Chapter 1: The Unintentional Hurt 33
    Chapter 2: The Weight of Unforgiveness 35
    Chapter 3: The Consequences of Resentment 37
Part 2: The Journey to Forgiveness 39
    Chapter 4: A Heart Open to God's Leading 41
    Chapter 5: Unshackling the Chains of Resentment 43
    Chapter 6: The Value of Perseverance 45
Part 3: Becoming a Gracious, Merciful and Forgiving Servant 47
    Chapter 7: Embracing Unconditional Forgiveness 49
    Chapter 8: Serving With Grace: Letting Go of Self 51
    Chapter 9: Mercy in Motion 53
Part 4: Restoring the Harmony 55
    Chapter 10: The Road to Recovery and Healing 57
    Chapter 11: Rebuilding Trust and Intimacy 59
    Chapter 12: The Triumph of God's Love and Grace 61

Devotionals 63
   Devotional 1: Reflecting God's Grace 65
   Devotional 2: The Liberating Power of Mercy 69
   Devotional 3: Forgiveness: The Key to Unlocking Love 73
Additional Prayers 77
   Prayer to Love the Lord 79
   Prayer to Love Others 80
   Prayer to See Others The Way God Sees Them 81
   Prayer to for a Deeper Relationship with the Lord 82
   Prayer to Reflect God's Heart 83
   A Prayer to Forgive Others 84
   Prayer for Forgiveness 85
   A Prayer to be Gracious to Others 86
   Prayer for God's Grace 87
   A Prayer to be Merciful to Others 88
   Prayer for God's Mercy 89
   Prayer for Those who Mistreat Us 90
   Prayer for Healing from Past Hurt 91
   Prayer to Be Set Free from Bitterness 92
   Prayer to Be Set Free from Resentment 93
   Prayer To Be Set Free From Fear 94
   Prayer for Marriage Restoration 95
   Prayer for Personal Growth and Development 96
   Prayer for Strength 97
   Prayer for Humility 98
   Prayer for Wisdom 99

Prayer for Protection.. 100
Prayer for Favor... 101
Conclusion.. 103
About the Author 107

"To forgive is to set a prisoner free and discover that the prisoner was you."

—Lewis B. Smedes

INTRODUCTION

Leah and Jake's marriage was once a beautiful symphony, filled with laughter, love, and harmony. But one fateful day, Leah's unintentional hurt pierced Jake's heart, shattering their blissful melody.

Leah's careless words, spoken in a moment of frustration, cut deep into Jake's soul. He became withdrawn, a stranger in their own home. The warmth of his embrace, the tenderness of his touch, and the comfort of his words were replaced with an icy silence.

Days turned into weeks, and weeks into months, with Jake refusing to forgive Leah. His fear of being hurt again became a heavy burden, weighing down their marriage. He prioritized everyone else's needs over Leah's, leaving her feeling neglected and unloved.

Despite her efforts to make amends, Jake continued to bring up the past, reopening the wounds Leah had desperately tried to heal. Her attempts to change and grow were met with skepticism as Jake struggled to trust her again.

As the months passed, Leah's heart grew increasingly bitter as her love and devotion remained unreciprocated. Despite this, she chose to be the bigger person, continuing to show Jake love and kindness even when it felt like hatred radiated from him. She clung to her faith, striving to be a godly wife and praying for a miracle to restore their marriage.

But the resentment Jake harbored became unbearable, and Leah contemplated divorce. She felt like she was walking alone in their marriage, carrying the weight of their relationship on her shoulders. Yet, in her heart, she knew that God didn't want her marriage to end in divorce. She believed that everything she faced was a lesson to be learned, an opportunity to grow her faith.

Leah held onto Romans 8:28, **"And we know that in all things God works for the good of those who love him, who have been called according to his purpose." (NIV).** She believed there was a purpose for her pain, a reason for the struggles she faced. With newfound determination, she committed to standing firm in her faith, trusting God to transform their marriage and heal Jake's heart.

Leah used to pray fervently for Jake to love and lead her, but those prayers seemed to go unanswered. One day, she heard a gentle whisper in her heart, *"Change your prayers, Leah. Ask that Jake love and follow the Lord, and he will learn to love and lead you as he should."* She took this newfound understanding to heart, embarking on a journey of prayer and fasting, pleading with the Lord to transform Jake's heart.

And then, something remarkable happened. Jake began to change. He started showing Leah love and affection, initially making small gestures but gradually increasing. Though the scars of his past hurt still lingered, Leah saw glimpses of the man she once knew, the one who had captivated her heart.

In moments of frustration, Leah would gently ask Jake, *"What if God treated you, the way you treated me? Wouldn't you want*

Him to forgive and love you unconditionally?" She longed for Jake to understand that forgiveness is fundamental to love, just as God freely forgives us. Leah's words planted seeds of conviction, and Jake began to see the parallel between his unforgiveness and God's mercy.

Leah continued to pray fervently for Jake's complete healing, hoping that the trauma of his past would be fully healed and their marriage would flourish once more. Though the road to recovery was long and winding, Leah held onto her faith, believing that God's love and grace would ultimately prevail.

WHAT IF GOD TREATED YOU, THE WAY YOU TREATED ME?

The question echoed in my mind, a gentle rebuke that pierced my heart. *What if God treated me, the way I treated others?* The thought sent a shiver down my spine.

As I reflected on my actions, I realized that I had been withholding forgiveness and love from those who had wronged me. I had been judging and condemning them as I often did with myself. But God doesn't treat me that way. When I sin, He doesn't withhold His love and forgiveness. Instead, He pours out His grace and mercy, inviting me to repent and return to Him.

If God treated me the way I treated others, I would be lost and condemned. But that's not how He works. He treats me with kindness, compassion, and patience. He sees my flaws and shortcomings, but He loves me anyway. He forgives me when I fail and helps me start anew.

As I reflected on this, I realized that I needed to change. I needed to extend the same grace and forgiveness to others that God extended to me. I needed to love and accept them, even when they failed. I needed to be a reflection of God's love and mercy in their lives.

The question, *"What if God treated you, the way you treated me?"* became a turning point for me. It reminded me that I am called to be a vessel of God's love and grace, not a judge and condemner. It taught me to forgive and love others, just as God forgives and loves me.

May we all learn to treat others the way God treats us; with love, mercy, and grace. May we be quick to forgive and slow to judge, just like our Heavenly Father. May we always remember that we all need His love and forgiveness every day.

FORGIVENESS, GRACE AND MERCY

What if God treated you, the way you treated others? This powerful and thought-provoking question challenges us to reflect on our actions and behavior. If we expect God's grace, mercy, and forgiveness, then we should extend the same to those around us. Consider how you have been treating others, especially those closest to you. Imagine if God treated you with the same level of kindness, understanding, and compassion—or lack thereof—that you have shown to others. How would you feel?

This question encourages us to examine our behavior, acknowledge shortcomings, and treat others with empathy, love, and grace—just as God treats us. It is a call to self-reflection, personal growth, and living with kindness and compassion towards all.

So what are forgiveness, grace, and mercy? Are they really that necessary? Do we really have to forgive, show grace, and offer mercy to those who hurt us? I mean, they clearly don't deserve it, right? WRONG.

To forgive means to let go of anger and resentment, releasing the hurt. Grace is unmerited favor and kindness extended by God or others, especially in times of need or difficulty. Mercy is showing compassion to someone who deserves punishment. Together, forgiveness, grace, and mercy form the cornerstone of the Christian faith, guiding believers to reflect God's love and compassion in their daily lives. Through forgiveness, believers experience the freedom of release from sin's bondage; by grace, they receive the unmerited gift of salvation, and with mercy, they find comfort and restoration in times of need. Embracing these principles, Christians are empowered to extend love, kindness, and compassion to others, reflecting the heart of God and illuminating the darkness with His transformative light.

So, how can you forgive those who have wronged you? How can you extend grace to those persons? How can you become a merciful servant of the Lord?

Here are some practical steps toward forgiveness, grace, and mercy:

Forgiveness

1. Recognize the hurt: Acknowledge the pain and hurt caused by others.

2. Let go of resentment: Choose to release the anger and bitterness.

3. Pray for the offender: Ask God to bless and forgive them.

4. Seek reconciliation: If possible, try to repair the relationship.

5. Remember God's forgiveness: Recall how God has forgiven you and extend the same grace to others.

Benefits of Forgiveness

- Freedom from resentment and anger.
- Peace and joy in our relationships.
- A deeper trust in God's sovereignty.
- A clearer conscience and a sense of integrity.
- A greater ability to love and serve others.

Barriers to Forgiveness

- Pride and a need for revenge.
- Persistent anger and bitterness.
- Doubt in God's sovereignty.
- Preoccupation with our rights and needs.
- A lack of understanding and empathy for others.

FORGIVENESS IS A CHOICE

Forgiveness is not a feeling but a choice. It is a decision to release the debt that someone owes us and to trust in God's justice and sovereignty. When we forgive, we open ourselves up to God's healing and restoration. This act brings freedom and peace as we let go of our burdens and give them to God.

Forgiveness is not always easy, but it is always worth it. It is a continual process that requires us to choose to forgive, even when it is difficult. Yet, as we persist in this choice, we experience the profound freedom and peace that come from entrusting our burdens to God.

Types of Forgiveness

There are three types of forgiveness:

1. Forgiveness of others: This is the most common type of forgiveness, and it involves releasing others from their debts to us.

2. Forgiveness of ourselves: This type of forgiveness involves releasing ourselves from our own guilt and shame.

3. Forgiveness of God: This type of forgiveness involves letting go of disappointment or frustration with the way

our lives have turned out and, instead, trusting that God has a purpose and plan.

Forgiveness is the radiant light that pierces the darkness of hurt and betrayal, illuminating the path to healing and redemption. It is the soothing balm that heals the wounds of our souls, restoring hope and renewing our spirit. Forgiveness is the liberating embrace that sets us free from the chains of resentment and anger, unleashing a torrent of love and mercy.

Forgiveness is a fundamental aspect of the Christian faith. In the story of Joseph (see Genesis 37-50), we see a powerful example of forgiveness in action. Joseph's brothers, who had sold him into slavery and left him for dead, went to Egypt seeking food during a famine. Now a powerful leader, Joseph could have easily sought revenge, but instead, he chose to forgive his brothers and welcome them into his life.

"You intended to harm me, but God intended it for good to accomplish what is now being done, the saving of many lives." (Genesis 50:20 – NIV).

This story shows that forgiveness is not just about the other person but about our own healing and freedom. When we choose to forgive, we release the hold that the other person has on us, opening ourselves up to God's healing and restoration.

By forgiving others, we reflect the very nature of God who has forgiven us through Jesus Christ. We experience the freedom and peace that come from releasing bitterness and anger, and we are able to move forward in our lives.

Forgiveness is the lifeblood of our souls, nourishing us with each passing moment. It is the gentle rain that quenches the parched earth of our hearts, reviving hope and renewal. With every choice to forgive, we breathe in the fresh air of freedom, unshackling ourselves from the weight of bitterness, resentment, and anger.

Forgiveness is the masterful brushstroke that paints a new canvas of hope and love. It is the symphony of grace that harmonizes the discord of our souls. Like the resplendent sunrise that banishes the night of hurt and fear, forgiveness brings light to our darkest moments.

It is the gentle whisper that soothes the turbulent waters of our hearts, calming the storms within. Forgiveness stands as the unshakeable foundation on which we build; it is a rock of hope and redemption guiding our path forward.

Extending Grace

1. Serve with humility: Put others' needs before your own.

2. Show compassion: Be gentle and caring.

3. Listen actively: Hear others' stories and struggles.

4. Offer forgiveness: Let go of grudges and resentments.

5. Pray for others: Intercede on their behalf.

6. Embrace humility: Recognize your own weaknesses and limitations.

7. Seek to understand: Ask questions and learn from others.

8. Be patient: Wait on God and trust in His timing.

9. Show love: Demonstrate God's love through your actions.

10. Seek guidance: Ask the Holy Spirit to guide you in your interactions with others.

Like the Good Samaritan (see Luke 10:25-37), we are called to extend grace to others. This parable teaches us that our neighbors are not just those we like or who are like us but also those who are different and in need. The lesson is clear: we must show mercy and compassion to all people, just as God has shown mercy and compassion to us.

Benefits of Serving with Grace

- Deeper relationships and connections.
- A greater sense of purpose and meaning.
- A clearer conscience and a sense of integrity.
- A greater ability to love and serve others.
- A deeper trust in God's sovereignty.

There are barriers to serving with grace, including:

- Pride and a need for control.
- A focus on our own needs and desires.
- Skepticism towards God's sovereignty.

- A fear of being taken advantage of.
- A lack of understanding and empathy for others.

May we embrace the call to serve with grace, and may our lives be marked by the beauty and power of grace.

Showing Mercy

1. Treat others with kindness: Show compassion and empathy.

2. Be understanding: Put yourself in others' shoes.

3. Offer help: Assist those in need.

4. Speak words of encouragement: Build others up.

5. Show hospitality: Welcome and include others.

In the Parable of the Prodigal Son (see Luke 15:11-32), a father's son squanders his inheritance and returns home in shame. Instead of scolding him, the father welcomes him back with open arms and throws a feast to celebrate his return.

God is like the father in the parable, welcoming us back with mercy and love when we turn away from our sins and return to Him. We are called to show others the same mercy and love, forgiving and welcoming them back when they fail.

Scripture Reference

"But the father said to his servants, 'Quick! Bring the best robe and put it on him. Put a ring on his finger and sandals

on his feet. Bring the fattened calf and kill it. Let's have a feast and celebrate. For this son of mine was dead and is alive again; he was lost and is found.' So they began to celebrate." (Luke 15:22-24 – NIV).

Benefits of Showing Mercy

- Deeper relationships and connections.
- A greater sense of purpose and meaning.
- A clearer conscience and a sense of integrity.
- A greater ability to love and serve others.
- Strengthened faith in God's sovereignty.

Barriers to Showing Mercy

- Pride and a need for justice.
- A focus on our own needs and desires.
- A feeling of uncertainty towards God's sovereignty.
- A fear of being taken advantage of.
- A lack of understanding and empathy for others.

Showing mercy is not just a choice; it is a command. It is not just a feeling; it is a commitment. It is not just for others; it is for ourselves. When we choose to show mercy, we open ourselves up to God's healing and restoration. We experience the freedom and peace that come from extending love and kindness to others.

Remember, forgiveness, grace, and mercy are not one-time actions but ongoing processes. By following these steps and seeking God's guidance, you can become a more forgiving, gracious, and merciful servant of the Lord.

PART 1

"THE SHATTERED MELODY"

"When the music of our lives is disrupted by the discords of hurt and betrayal, forgiveness is the harmonizer that restores the melody of our soul."

—Anonymous

Chapter 1

The Unintentional Hurt

Leah's careless words pierced Jake's heart, shattering their blissful melody. This unintentional hurt led to a downward spiral of unforgiveness, resentment, and a broken marriage.

As we navigate the complexities of relationships, we often underestimate the power of our words and actions. However, the truth is that our words have the power to either build up or tear down those around us.

In the book of Proverbs, we are reminded that **"the tongue has the power of life and death, and those who love it will eat its fruit." (Proverbs 18:21 – NIV).** This scripture highlights the significance of our words and the impact they have on others.

Leah and Jake's story serves as a poignant reminder of the devastating effects of unintentional hurt. A careless comment, a thoughtless action, and a once beautiful marriage was left in shambles. But it is not too late to change. We can learn to be more mindful of our words and actions, think before speaking, and choose love and kindness over hurt and anger.

In Proverbs 12:18, we are encouraged to choose our words wisely, as **"The words of the reckless pierce like swords, but the tongue of the wise brings healing." (NIV).** This scripture reminds us that our words have the power to either hurt or heal.

Let's strive to be wise in our words, bringing life and love to those around us. Let's choose to build each other up rather than tear each other down. Let's create a culture of kindness, compassion, and love where our words bring healing and restoration to those around us.

Chapter 2

The Weight of Unforgiveness

Jake's fear of being hurt again became a heavy burden, weighing down their marriage. His refusal to forgive Leah led to a toxic environment of resentment and anger, causing their relationship to crumble. Unforgiveness is a weight that we do not have to carry; God invites us to lay our burdens at His feet.

In Matthew 6:14-15, Jesus teaches us, **"For if you forgive other people when they sin against you, your heavenly Father will also forgive you. But if you do not forgive others their sins, Your Father will not forgive your sins." (NIV).** Forgiveness is not just about the other person; it is about us. It is about releasing the hold that unforgiveness has on our hearts and minds.

Matthew 11:28-30 says, **"Come to me, all you who are weary and burdened, and I will give you rest. Take my yoke upon you and learn from me, for I am gentle and humble in heart, and you will find rest for your souls. For my yoke is easy and my burden is light." (NIV).** Jesus invites us to come to Him with our burdens, including the weight of unforgiveness. He promises to give us rest and to help us carry our loads because His yoke is easy, and His burden is light.

When we refuse to forgive, we carry a heavy burden that weighs us down and prevents us from moving forward. But when we release our burdens to God, we find freedom and rest. Let's choose to forgive, not for the sake of others, but for our own sake. Let's release the weight of unforgiveness and find rest in God's love and grace.

Chapter 3

The Consequences of Resentment

Jake's resentment became unbearable, and Leah found herself contemplating divorce. Resentment is a poison that eats away at our hearts, causing us to become bitter and hardened. We must recognize the danger of resentment and choose to release it, allowing God to heal our wounds and restore our relationships.

Resentment is a slow-burning fire that consumes our hearts and minds. It is a poison that seeps into our souls, causing us to become bitter and hardened. It is a trap that we easily fall into, but it is a trap that we can escape. Hebrews 12:15 warns us, **"See to it that no one falls short of the grace of God and that no bitter root grows up to cause trouble and defile many." (NIV).** Resentment is a bitter root that can grow deep and strong, causing trouble and defiling many, but we don't have to let it.

Ephesians 4:31-32 says, **"Get rid of all bitterness, rage and anger, brawling and slander, along with every form of malice. Be kind and compassionate to one another, forgiving each other, just as in Christ God forgave you." (NIV).** This scripture warns us of the dangers of resentment and its effects on our hearts and relationships. We are called to discard bitterness, rage, and anger and instead embrace kindness, compassion, and forgiveness.

When we choose to hold onto resentment, we become trapped in a cycle of bitterness and anger. We become unable to move forward, and our relationships suffer. But when we release resentment and choose forgiveness, we find freedom and rest. We can learn to forgive and find peace in God's love.

Leah and Jake's story teaches us that forgiveness is not always easy, but it is necessary for our own healing and freedom. By choosing forgiveness, we release resentment's hold on our hearts and minds, opening ourselves up to God's healing and restoration. This allows Him to work in our lives in a powerful way, transforming us and our relationships.

We can break free from the cycle of resentment and find healing in God's love. By embracing forgiveness and kindness, we can create a culture of love and compassion where our relationships can thrive and grow. May we choose to release resentment and find peace in God's grace.

PART 2

THE JOURNEY TO FORGIVENESS

"Forgiveness has the power to heal, unforgiveness has the power to destroy."

— Cheleta Buddo-Gayle

Chapter 4

A Heart Open to God's Leading

Leah's journey towards forgiveness and restoration was transformative, requiring her to confront the depths of her pain and trust in God's goodness. As she opened her heart to God's leading, she began to see the beauty of forgiveness and the freedom it brings.

Forgiveness is not just about the other person; it is about us. It is about releasing resentment's hold on our hearts and minds, and allowing God to heal our wounds.

When we choose to forgive, we open ourselves up to God's healing and restoration. We allow Him to work in our lives in a powerful way, bringing freedom and love to our relationships. As Psalm 32:8 reminds us, **"I will instruct you and teach you in the way you should go; I will counsel you with my loving eye on you." (NIV).** God desires to guide us and teach us in the way we should go. He promises to counsel us with His loving eye on us, leading us on a path of forgiveness and restoration.

As we navigate the journey of forgiveness, we must keep our hearts open to God's leading. We must be willing to listen to His gentle whisper, guiding us towards love and compassion. We must trust in His power and love, knowing He desires to heal our wounds and restore our relationships. By doing so, we will experience the power of forgiveness in a new way and discover a freedom and healing that we never thought possible.

Chapter 5

Unshackling the Chains of Resentment

Resentment can be a stubborn companion, clinging to our hearts and minds like a shadow. It whispers lies of hurt and betrayal, fueling our anger and bitterness, but God's truth shines brighter, illuminating a path to freedom and forgiveness.

Leah's journey shows us that resentment's grip can be loosened. As she chose to forgive Jake, she discovered a strength she never knew she had. Forgiveness became her lifeline, pulling her out of the quicksand of resentment and into the solid ground of restoration.

What would happen if we released resentment and extended love and kindness instead? Would we find freedom from the weight of bitterness and anger? Would we discover a new path that leads to healing and restoration? Romans 12:21 reminds us, **"Do not be overcome by evil, but overcome evil with good." (NIV).** We can choose to respond with love and forgiveness instead of resentment and anger. We can overcome the evil of resentment with the good of forgiveness and find freedom and healing in the process.

As we release resentment, we create space for God's love and grace to flow in. We begin to see the beauty of forgiveness, the freedom it brings, and the hope it offers. Breaking free from resentment's grip allows us to discover a new way of living filled with love, joy, and peace.

Chapter 6

The Value of Perseverance

Leah's journey towards forgiveness and restoration wasn't easy, but it proved to be immensely rewarding. She persevered through the pain and hurt, trusting in God's power and love to heal and restore her. In doing so, she discovered a strength she never knew she possessed.

Perseverance is a valuable virtue in our walk with God. It is the ability to endure difficult circumstances, trusting in His goodness and love. It is the willingness to keep moving forward, even when the road ahead seems uncertain.

James 1:2-4 reminds us, **"Consider it pure joy, my brothers and sisters, whenever you face trials of many kinds, because you know that the testing of your faith produces perseverance. Let perseverance finish its work so that you may be mature and complete, not lacking anything." (NIV).** We can choose to see our trials and difficulties as opportunities to grow and persevere. As we do, we become mature and complete, lacking nothing. We develop a deeper trust in God, a stronger faith, and a more compassionate heart.

Perseverance is not merely about enduring difficult times but about growing and learning from them. It is about becoming the person God created us to be and experiencing the abundant life He has for us. Leah's story teaches us that perseverance is crucial for forgiveness and restoration. We must be willing to keep moving forward, even when the pain and hurt feel overwhelming. Trusting in God's power and love, we know that He is working all things for our good.

PART 3

BECOMING A GRACIOUS, MERCIFUL AND FORGIVING SERVANT

"Blessed are the merciful, for they will be shown mercy." (Matthew 5:7 – NIV).

Chapter 7

Embracing Unconditional Forgiveness

Leah's journey towards forgiveness was transformative, teaching her the true meaning of unconditional forgiveness. She learned that forgiveness is about releasing others from their debts and freeing ourselves from the burden of resentment. Embracing unconditional forgiveness, she discovered a sense of liberation and peace that she had never known before.

Forgiveness is a process, and it is not always easy. It requires us to let go of our need for justice and our desire for revenge. It demands that we trust God's sovereignty and plan for our lives. Yet, the freedom and peace that come from forgiveness are worth the struggle. Ephesians 4:32 reminds us, **"Be kind and compassionate to one another, forgiving each other, just as in Christ God forgave you." (NIV).** This scripture teaches us that forgiveness is a fundamental aspect of our faith. Just as God has forgiven us, we are called to forgive others.

Leah's story teaches us that forgiveness is a continuous process, not a one-time event. It requires us to continually choose to forgive, even when it is hard. As we do, we experience the freedom and peace that come from releasing our burdens to God. Forgiveness isn't solely about others; it profoundly impacts our relationship with God. By forgiving, we draw closer to Him and encounter His love and grace more deeply.

Moreover, forgiveness liberates us from the chains of bitterness and resentment. Clinging to grudges and unforgiveness can consume our thoughts and emotions, trapping us in a cycle of negativity and hurt. When we choose to forgive, we break free from this cycle and embrace the joy and peace of a life rooted in love and grace.

Chapter 8

Serving With Grace: Letting Go of Self

Leah's journey toward forgiveness and serving with grace is a powerful reminder that serving others is not just about what we do but why we do it. When we serve with selfless love, we demonstrate the love of Christ in our lives. 1 John 3:16 says, **"This is how we know what love is: Jesus Christ laid down his life for us. And we ought to lay down our lives for our brothers and sisters." (NIV).** This scripture teaches us that serving with grace requires us to let go of our need for control and our desire for recognition.

Leah's story teaches us that serving with grace is not just about our actions but our motivations. When we serve with selfless love, we can put the needs of others before our own and demonstrate the love of Christ in our lives. Serving gracefully requires us to have faith in God's divine guidance and His perfect plan for our lives. It requires us to let go of our own agenda and our desire for control, allowing God to work through us to bless others.

In addition, serving with grace allows us to experience the joy and fulfillment that comes from living a life of love and service. When we serve others with selfless love, we can experience Christ's love in a deeper way and draw closer to God. We are also able to build stronger relationships with others and create a ripple effect of love and kindness in our communities.

Serving with grace is not just about what we do; it is about why we do it. When we serve with selfless love, we are able to demonstrate the love of Christ in our lives and experience the joy and fulfillment that comes from living a life of love and service.

Chapter 9

Mercy in Motion

Leah's journey toward forgiveness and her demonstration of grace and mercy in action serves as a powerful reminder that mercy is not merely a feeling but an action. It is a deliberate choice to extend love and kindness to others, even when they don't deserve it. Matthew 5:7 says, **"Blessed are the merciful, for they will be shown mercy." (NIV).** This scripture teaches us that mercy is a fundamental aspect of our faith. When we show mercy to others, we experience the mercy of God in our own lives.

Leah's story teaches us that mercy is not just about what we do but about why we do it. When we show mercy with a humble and loving heart, we demonstrate the love of Christ in our lives. Mercy is not just about feeling sorry for someone; it is about taking action to help them in their time of need, extending love and kindness to others, even when they don't deserve it.

Showing mercy in motion allows us to create a culture of love and kindness in our communities, inspiring others to do the same. It also helps us build stronger relationships and experience the joy of living a life of love and service.

Mercy in motion is not just a feeling; it is a choice to extend love and kindness to others, demonstrating the love of Christ and finding fulfillment in serving others.

PART 4

RESTORING THE HARMONY

"Blessed are the peacemakers, for they will be called children of God." (Matthew 5:9 – NIV).

Chapter 10

The Road to Recovery and Healing

Leah's journey toward forgiveness, serving with grace, and showing mercy led her to a deeper understanding of the need for recovery and healing. She realized that the wounds of the past don't just disappear; they need to be treated and healed. As Psalm 147:3 reminds us, **"He heals the brokenhearted and binds up their wounds." (NIV).** God is our Healer and Restorer, and He desires to heal our wounds and restore us to wholeness.

Leah's story teaches us that recovery and healing require us to confront our wounds rather than hide or deny them. We must acknowledge the pain and hurt and seek help and support from others. Recovery and healing are not just destinations; they are ongoing journeys that entail confronting our wounds, seeking support, and trusting in God's sovereignty. When we choose to recover and heal, we open ourselves up to God's healing and restoration, experiencing the freedom and peace that come from releasing our burdens to Him.

This journey of recovery and healing isn't always easy. It demands courage, vulnerability, and a willingness to confront our deepest fears and insecurities. But the reward is profound: a deeper understanding of ourselves, a stronger faith, and a more compassionate heart. As we traverse the road to recovery and healing, we can trust that God is with us every step of the way, guiding, supporting, and loving us unconditionally.

Chapter 11

Rebuilding Trust and Intimacy

Leah's journey toward recovery and healing led her to a deeper understanding of the need to rebuild trust and intimacy in her relationships. She realized that trust is not just a feeling but a choice—a deliberate decision to believe in someone's goodness and reliability. Intimacy is not just physical but emotional and spiritual as well—a deep connection with someone that transcends words and actions.

As 1 Corinthians 13:7 reminds us, **"Love bears all things, believes all things, hopes all things, endures all things." (ESV).** Love is not just a feeling but a choice—a choice to believe in someone, to hope for someone, and to endure with someone through thick and thin. Trust is a fundamental aspect of love.

Leah's story teaches us that rebuilding trust and intimacy requires us to be vulnerable, transparent, and honest. We need to communicate openly and honestly with each other and seek to understand each other's perspectives and feelings. We must be willing to listen, forgive, and work through conflicts together. Rebuilding trust and intimacy is not just a destination; it is a journey of love, forgiveness, and growth.

As we walk this journey, we can trust that God is with us, guiding and supporting us every step of the way. He desires for us to have deep, meaningful relationships with others, and He is always working to restore and redeem our relationships, just as He restores and redeems us.

Chapter 12

The Triumph of God's Love and Grace

Through Leah's story, we learn that the power of God's love and grace is unleashed when we surrender to His sovereign control and trust in His plan for our lives. We need to surrender our fears, doubts, and worries to God and trust that He is always working for our good. The triumph of God's love and grace is not just a destination but a journey of trust, surrender, and transformation. When we trust God's sovereignty, we open ourselves up to a deeper relationship with Him and others. We experience the freedom and peace that come from releasing our burdens to God and discover the transformative power of His love and grace in our lives.

As Romans 8:37-39 reminds us, **"No, in all these things we are more than conquerors through him who loved us. For I am convinced that neither death nor life, neither angels nor demons, neither the present nor the future, nor any powers, neither height nor depth, nor anything else in all creation, will be able to separate us from the love of God that is in Christ Jesus our Lord." (NIV).** This scripture assures us that God's love is not just a feeling but a choice—an unwavering, unrelenting, and unbreakable love, and nothing can separate us from His love.

In the end, Leah's story is a testament to the triumph of God's love and grace. It shows us that no matter what we have been through or what wounds we may carry, God's love and grace can heal, restore, and transform us. It reminds us that we are not alone on this journey—God is with us every step of the way, guiding, supporting, and loving us unconditionally.

DEVOTIONALS

Devotional 1

Reflecting God's Grace

Story

Michelle was struggling to forgive her friend who had betrayed her trust. She felt hurt and angry and didn't know how to move forward. Then, she had a realization: God had forgiven her of much more than what her friend had done against her. Inspired by this, she decided to extend grace to her friend, just as God had extended grace to her. As she did, she felt a weight lift off her shoulders, and their relationship began to heal.

God's Grace

God's grace is a gift that we don't deserve, but He gives it to us anyway. It is His unconditional love and forgiveness extended to us through Jesus Christ. When we accept His grace, we are freed from the chains of sin and shame and empowered to live a new life.

Bible Scriptures to Meditate On

Ephesians 2:8-9 – **"For it is by grace you have been saved, through faith— and this is not from yourselves, it is the gift of God—not by works, so that no one can boast." (NIV).**

Lesson

God's grace is a gift that we can't earn or deserve. It is a free gift, given to us through faith in Jesus Christ.

Romans 5:8 – **"But God demonstrates his own love for us in this: While we were still sinners, Christ died for us." (NIV).**

Lesson

God's grace is demonstrated through His love for us, even when we were still sinners. He loved us enough to send His Son to die for us.

2 Corinthians 12:9 – **"But he said to me, 'My grace is sufficient for you, for my power is made perfect in weakness.' Therefore I will boast all the more gladly about my weaknesses, so that Christ's power may rest on me."** (NIV).

Lesson

God's grace is sufficient for us, even in our weaknesses. His power is made perfect in our weakness, and He uses our weaknesses to show His strength.

Conclusion

As we reflect on God's grace in our lives, let us remember to extend that same grace to others. Just as God has forgiven us, we should forgive others. Just as God has shown us love and compassion, we should show love and compassion to others.

Reflections

- How have you experienced God's grace in your life?
- Who do you need to extend grace to today?
- How can you show God's love and compassion to those around you?

Action Steps

- Write down ways you have experienced God's grace in your life.
- Pray for the strength to extend grace to someone who has hurt you.
- Look for opportunities to show God's love and compassion to those around you.

Prayer

Dear God, thank You for Your grace and love towards me. Help me extend that same grace to others so they may see Your love and compassion through me.

In Jesus' name, I pray. Amen.

Devotional 2

The Liberating Power of Mercy

Story

Elaine had been holding onto resentment towards her cousin for years until she realized that her unforgiveness was only hurting herself. She decided to extend mercy to her cousin, and as she did, a heavy burden was lifted from her heart. She was finally free from the chains of bitterness and resentment.

God's Mercy

God's mercy is His unconditional love and compassion towards us, even when we don't deserve it. He is slow to anger and abounds in love, and He desires to show us mercy and forgiveness.

Bible Scriptures to Meditate On

Psalm 136:1-3 – **"Give thanks to the Lord, for he is good, for his steadfast love endures forever! Give thanks to the God of gods, for his steadfast love endures forever! Give thanks to the Lord of lords, for his steadfast love endures forever!"** (ESV).

Lesson

God's mercy and love endures forever, and we can always count on His compassion and forgiveness.

Matthew 5:7 – **"Blessed are the merciful, for they shall receive mercy."** (ESV).

Lesson

When we extend mercy to others, we will also receive mercy from God and others.

Luke 17:19 – **"Then he said to him, 'Rise and go; your faith has made you well.'" (NIV).**

Lesson

Jesus showed mercy to those who came to Him, and He healed them physically and spiritually. We can come to Him with our brokenness and receive His mercy and healing.

Conclusion

As we reflect on God's mercy in our lives, let us remember to extend that same mercy to others. Just as God has shown us compassion and forgiveness, we should show compassion and forgiveness to others.

Reflections

- How have you experienced God's mercy in your life?
- Who do you need to extend mercy to today?
- How can you show God's love and compassion to those around you?

Action Steps

- Write down ways you have experienced God's mercy in your life.
- Pray for the strength to extend mercy to someone who has hurt you.

- Look for opportunities to show God's love and compassion to those around you.

Prayer

Dear God, thank You for Your mercy and love towards me. Help me extend that same mercy to others, so that they may experience Your healing and compassion through me.

In Jesus' name, I pray. Amen.

Devotional 3

Forgiveness: The Key to Unlocking Love

Story

Crystal had been holding onto resentment towards her husband for years, until she realized that her unforgiveness was only hurting their relationship. She decided to forgive him, and as she did, the tension melted away. Their love and intimacy were restored, and their relationship was stronger than ever.

God's Forgiveness

God's forgiveness is His unconditional love and mercy towards us, even when we don't deserve it. He desires to forgive us and restore our relationship with Him, and He calls us to do the same with others.

Bible Scriptures to Meditate On

Matthew 6:14-15 – **"For if you forgive other people when they sin against you, your heavenly Father will also forgive you. But if you do not forgive others their sins, your Father will not forgive your sins." (NIV).**

Lesson

Forgiveness is a fundamental aspect of our relationship with God and with others. When we choose to forgive, we open ourselves up to receiving God's forgiveness and love.

Ephesians 4:32 – **"Be kind and compassionate to one another, forgiving each other, just as in Christ God forgave you." (NIV).**

Lesson

Forgiveness is an act of kindness and compassion towards others, just as God has shown us kindness and compassion through His forgiveness.

1 John 1:9 – **"If we confess our sins, he is faithful and just and will forgive us our sins and purify us from all unrighteousness." (NIV).**

Lesson

When we confess our sins and choose to forgive others, God is faithful and just to forgive us and purify us from all unrighteousness.

Conclusion

Forgiveness is the key to unlocking love in our relationships. When we choose to forgive, we create a safe and loving environment where love and intimacy can flourish.

Reflections

- What are some areas in your life where you need to practice forgiveness?
- How can you show kindness and compassion to someone who has hurt you?
- What are some ways you can confess your sins and receive God's forgiveness and purification?

Action Steps

- Write down the name of someone you need to forgive and pray for the strength to do so.
- Look for opportunities to show kindness and compassion to those around you.
- Confess your sins to God and receive His forgiveness and purification.

Prayer

Dear God, thank You for Your forgiveness and love towards me. Help me extend that same forgiveness to others so that our relationships may be a testament to Your power and love.

In Jesus' name, I pray. Amen.

ADDITIONAL PRAYERS

Prayer to Love the Lord

Dear Heavenly Father,

I come before You, desiring to love You more deeply and fully. Help me surrender my heart and life to You so that I may love You with all my heart, soul, mind, and strength.

As Your Word says in Mark 12:30, **"Love the Lord your God with all your heart and with all your soul and with all your mind and with all your strength." (NIV).**

I pray that You would fill me with Your love, that I may love You in return. Help me to seek You above all else, to delight in Your presence, and to find joy in Your love.

Let my love for You be evident in my thoughts, words, and actions. May I be a reflection of Your love to those around me, and may my life be a testimony to the power of Your love.

In Jesus' name, I pray. Amen.

Prayer to Love Others

Dear Heavenly Father,

Help me to love others as You have loved me. Let my heart be filled with Your love so I may extend kindness, compassion, and grace to those around me.

As Your Word says in John 13:34, **"A new command I give you: Love one another. As I have loved you, so you must love one another."** (NIV).

I pray to be a true reflection of Your love, Lord, in all my interactions. Please grant me the virtues of patience, understanding, and selflessness. Guide me to see others through Your compassionate eyes, loving them as You do.

Let my love for others be a testimony to Your love, and may it bring glory to Your name. Help me to love without condition, to forgive freely, and to serve humbly.

In Jesus' name, I pray. Amen.

Prayer to See Others The Way God Sees Them

Dear God,

I come to You today asking for eyes to see others as You see them - with love, compassion, and grace. Help me to look beyond the exterior and see the beauty, worth, and potential in each person.

As Your Word says in 1 Samuel 16:7 (NIV), **"The Lord does not look at the things people look at. People look at the outward appearance, but the Lord looks at the heart."**

Change my perspective, Lord, and give me a heart that loves and accepts others as You do. May I see the image of God in every person, and may my interactions with them be filled with kindness, understanding, and empathy.

In Jesus' name, I pray. Amen.

Prayer to for a Deeper Relationship with the Lord

Dear God,

I come to You today longing to deepen my relationship with You. I desire to know You more intimately, to love You more passionately, and to serve You more faithfully.

As Your Word says in Psalm 119:10 (NIV), **"I seek you with all my heart; do not let me stray from your commands."**

Help me to seek You with all my heart, to crave Your presence, and to abide in Your love. May my soul be anchored in Your truth, and may my spirit be refreshed by Your grace.

Draw me closer to Your heart, Lord, and reveal Yourself to me in ways I've never known before. May my prayers be more than just words, but a genuine conversation with You, my Heavenly Father.

Show me the depths of Your love, the heights of Your glory, and the breadth of Your grace. May my life be a testament to Your goodness, and may my heart be forever changed by Your presence.

In Jesus' name, I pray. Amen.

Prayer to Reflect God's Heart

Dear God,

I come to You today desiring to reflect Your heart in every aspect of my life. Help me to love as You love, to forgive as You forgive, and to show grace as You show grace.

As Your Word says in 2 Corinthians 5:20 (NIV), **"We are therefore Christ's ambassadors, as though God were making his appeal through us."**

Make me a vessel of Your love, a conduit of Your grace, and a reflection of Your character. May my thoughts, words, and actions be a testament to Your goodness and mercy.

May I be a source of comfort, hope, and light in the darkness. May my heart be transformed to resemble Yours, and may my life be a reflection of Your love and grace.

In Jesus' name, I pray. Amen.

A Prayer to Forgive Others

Dear Heavenly Father,

I struggle with forgiving those who have hurt me, but I know that You command me to forgive as You have forgiven me. Help me to release the bitterness and anger in my heart and choose to forgive others just as You have forgiven me.

As Your Word says in Matthew 6:14-15 – **"For if you forgive other people when they sin against you, your heavenly Father will also forgive you. But if you do not forgive others their sins, your Father will not forgive your sins."** (NIV).

I choose to forgive *[name]* for *[specific hurt or offense]*. I release them from any debt they owe me and pray that You would bless them and bring them closer to You.

Thank You for Your example of forgiveness on the cross and for the grace to forgive others. Help me to continue to walk in forgiveness and freedom.

In Jesus' name, I pray. Amen.

Prayer for Forgiveness

Dear Heavenly Father,

I come before You with a humble heart, seeking Your forgiveness for my sins. I am sorry for the times I have failed You and turned away from Your love. Please forgive me for my mistakes and wash me clean with Your mercy.

As Your Word says in 1 John 1:9, **"If we confess our sins, he is faithful and just and will forgive us our sins and purify us from all unrighteousness." (NIV).**

I now confess my sins to You, Lord, and ask for Your forgiveness. Help me turn away from my sinful ways and walk in Your righteousness. Thank You for Your love and grace that forgives me and sets me free.

In Jesus' name, I pray. Amen.

A Prayer to be Gracious to Others

Dear Heavenly Father,

Help me to be gracious and kind to those around me, just as You have been gracious and kind to me. Let my words and actions be marked by love, compassion, and understanding.

As Your Word says in Ephesians 4:32, **"Be kind and compassionate to one another, forgiving each other, just as in Christ God forgave you."** (NIV).

I pray that I will be a reflection of Your grace and mercy and that my interactions with others will be a blessing to them. Please help me be slow to speak, quick to listen, and always seek to understand and show empathy.

May my heart be filled with Your love and my life be a testimony to Your grace. Let me be a source of encouragement and hope to those around me.

In Jesus' name, I pray. Amen.

Prayer for God's Grace

Dear Heavenly Father,

I come before You humbly, acknowledging my need for Your grace in every area of my life. Please pour out Your grace upon me so that I may know Your love and mercy in a deeper way.

As Your Word says in 2 Corinthians 9:8, **"And God is able to bless you abundantly, so that in all things at all times, having all that you need, you will abound in every good work." (NIV).**

I ask for Your grace to abound in my life so that I may be strengthened in my weaknesses and empowered to live a life that honors You. Please help me trust in Your goodness and provision and rest in Your grace, which is sufficient for me.

Thank You for Your unfailing love and grace that saves, sustains, and empowers me to live for You. May Your grace be my guide, comfort, and hope.

In Jesus' name, I pray. Amen.

A Prayer to be Merciful to Others

Dear Heavenly Father,

Help me to be merciful to others, just as You have been merciful to me. Let my heart be filled with compassion, kindness, and understanding towards those who are struggling or hurting.

As Your Word says in Matthew 5:7, **"Blessed are the merciful, for they will be shown mercy." (NIV).**

I pray that I will be a reflection of Your mercy and that my interactions with others will be marked by grace and compassion. Please help me to be patient, forgiving, and understanding and to always seek to show mercy to those in need.

May my life be a testimony to Your mercy and a source of hope and comfort to those around me. Let me never forget the mercy You have shown me, and help me to extend that same mercy to others.

In Jesus' name, I pray. Amen.

Prayer for God's Mercy

Dear Heavenly Father,

I come before You, humbly seeking Your mercy and grace. I need Your loving-kindness and compassion, and I ask that You pour out Your mercy upon me.

As Your Word says in Psalm 136:1-3, **"Give thanks to the Lord, for he is good. His love endures forever! Give thanks to the God of gods. His love endures forever! Give thanks to the Lord of lords. His love endures forever!"** (NIV).

I thank You for Your enduring love and mercy that never fails. Help me trust in Your goodness and provision, and rest in Your new mercy every morning.

Show me Your mercy, Lord, and guide me on the path of righteousness. Forgive me for my sins, and help me to forgive others. Let Your mercy be my comfort, hope, and strength.

In Jesus' name, I pray. Amen.

Prayer for Those who Mistreat Us

Dear God,

I come to You today with a heart that's been hurt by the actions of others. I pray for those who have mistreated me, persecuted me, or sought to harm me.

As Your Word says in Matthew 5:44 (NIV), **"But I tell you, love your enemies and pray for those who persecute you."**

Help me to love as You love, to forgive as You forgive, and to pray for those who have hurt me. May my heart be free from bitterness, anger, and resentment.

Show me how to bless those who curse me, to pray for those who mistreat me, and to love those who seek to harm me. May my response to their actions be a testament to Your grace and mercy.

Change the hearts of those who have hurt me, Lord, and may they come to know Your love and forgiveness. May Your love and grace be the balm that heals our wounds and restores our relationships.

In Jesus' name, I pray. Amen.

Prayer for Healing from Past Hurt

Dear God,

I come to You with a heart that has been wounded and scarred from past experiences. I ask for Your healing touch to restore, renew, and set me free from the pain and hurt that still lingers. Please help me to release the bitterness and anger and to forgive those who have caused me harm. Let Your love and grace pour over me, and may Your peace that surpasses all understanding guard my heart and mind.

As it is written in Psalm 34:18, **"The Lord is near to the brokenhearted and saves the crushed in spirit." (ESV).** I claim this promise, Lord, and trust in Your goodness and love for me.

In Jesus' name, I pray. Amen.

Prayer to Be Set Free from Bitterness

Dear God,

I come before You today, acknowledging the bitterness that has taken root in my heart. I confess that I have held onto resentment and anger for far too long, and it has only brought me pain and suffering.

Your Word says in Ephesians 4:31-32, **"Get rid of all bitterness, rage and anger, brawling and slander, along with every form of malice. Be kind and compassionate to one another, forgiving each other, just as in Christ God forgave you." (NIV).**

I ask that You please forgive me for allowing bitterness to consume me. Please help me to release all resentment and anger and to forgive those who have wronged me. Show me how to extend kindness and compassion to others, just as You have extended it to me.

Lord, I pray that You will set me free from the chains of bitterness and fill me with Your love and grace. May Your power transform my heart, and may I be a vessel of Your mercy and forgiveness to others.

In Jesus' name, I pray. Amen.

Prayer to Be Set Free from Resentment

Dear God,

I come before You today, acknowledging the resentment that has taken hold of my heart. I confess that I have held onto grudges and hurts for far too long, and it has only brought me pain and suffering.

Your Word says in Matthew 6:14-15 – **"For if you forgive other people when they sin against you, your heavenly Father will also forgive you. But if you do not forgive others their sins, your Father will not forgive your sins." (NIV).**

I ask that You please forgive me for allowing resentment to consume me. Please help me to release all grudges and hurts and forgive those who have wronged me. Show me how to extend mercy and grace to others, just as You have extended it to me.

Lord, I pray that You would set me free from the chains of resentment and fill me with Your love and peace. May Your power transform my heart, and may I be a vessel of Your forgiveness and grace to others.

In Jesus' name, I pray. Amen.

Prayer To Be Set Free From Fear

Dear God,

I come to You today asking for freedom from fear. Fear that has held me back, fear that has stolen my peace and robbed me of rest.

Your Word says in 2 Timothy 1:7 (NIV), **"For God has not given me a spirit of fear, but of power and of love and of a sound mind."** I claim this promise today, and I ask that You would deliver me from the grip of fear.

Help me to trust in Your goodness, Your sovereignty, and Your love. May Your perfect love cast out all fear (1 John 4:18, NIV).

Set me free, Lord, from the chains of fear. Give me courage, strength, and wisdom to face whatever challenges come my way.

In Jesus' name, I pray. Amen.

Prayer for Marriage Restoration

Dear God,

I come to You today with a humble heart, asking for Your guidance and restoration in my marriage. I know that Your plans for us are for good and not for harm, and I trust in your ability to heal and restore our relationship.

As Your Word says in Ephesians 5:25-33 (NIV), **"Husbands, love your wives, just as Christ loved the church and gave himself up for her...,"** I ask that You would help us to love each other with the same selfless and sacrificial love that Christ has shown us.

Help us to communicate with kindness, to listen with understanding, and to forgive with grace. May our love be strengthened, our trust be rebuilt, and our union be made stronger.

Show us how to love each other as You have loved us, with patience, kindness, and selflessness. May our marriage be a testimony to Your power and grace.

In Jesus' name, I pray. Amen.

Prayer for Personal Growth and Development

Dear God,

I come to You today desiring to grow and flourish in every area of my life. Help me to embrace Your plan for my life, and may Your guidance and wisdom shape me into the person You intend me to be.

As Your Word says in Philippians 1:9-11 (NIV), **"And this is my prayer: that your love may abound more and more in knowledge and depth of insight, so that you may be able to discern what is best and may be pure and blameless for the day of Christ, filled with the fruit of righteousness that comes through Jesus Christ—to the glory and praise of God."**

Help me to discern what is best, to be pure and blameless, and to bear fruit in righteousness. May Your love and grace abound in me, and may I grow in knowledge and insight, becoming more like You each day.

Develop in me a heart of humility, a spirit of discipline, and a mind of clarity. May my thoughts, words, and actions honor You, and may I become a reflection of Your character and love.

In Jesus' name, I pray. Amen.

Prayer for Strength

Dear Heavenly Father,

I come before You, feeling weak and weary. I need Your strength to face the challenges ahead. Please pour out Your power and grace upon me that I may be empowered to overcome.

As Your Word says in Philippians 4:13, **"I can do all this through him who gives me strength." (NIV).**

I claim this promise, Lord, and ask that You fill me with Your mighty strength. Please help me trust in Your power and lean on You when I am weak. Let Your strength be my guide, comfort, and hope.

Please give me the strength to follow You, to serve You, and to glorify You in all I do. Let me be a reflection of Your power and grace, and may my life be a testimony to Your strength in me.

In Jesus' name, I pray. Amen.

Prayer for Humility

Dear Heavenly Father,

Help me to humble myself before You and others. May my heart be filled with a spirit of humility so that I may see myself as You see me and walk in humility and grace.

As Your Word says in Philippians 2:3-4, **"Do nothing out of selfish ambition or vain conceit. Rather, in humility, value others above yourselves, not looking to your own interests but each of you to the interests of the others." (NIV).**

I pray that I would put aside pride and self-importance and instead seek to serve and uplift others. Please help me be willing to listen, learn, grow, and always seek Your glory above my own.

Let my humility be a reflection of Your character, and may it bring glory to Your name. Please help me to be a servant-leader and to use my gifts and talents for the benefit of others.

In Jesus' name, I pray. Amen.

Prayer for Wisdom

Dear Heavenly Father,

I come before You, seeking wisdom and guidance. Please help me to discern Your will and to walk in Your ways.

As Your Word says in James 1:5, **"If any of you lacks wisdom, you should ask God, who gives generously to all without finding fault, and it will be given to you."** (NIV).

I pray that You would grant me wisdom beyond my own understanding, that I may make decisions that honor You and bring glory to Your name. Help me see things from Your perspective and to trust in Your sovereignty.

Let Your wisdom guide me in all aspects of my life so that I may be a light in the darkness and a source of hope for those around me. May Your wisdom be my comfort, guide, and strength.

In Jesus' name, I pray. Amen.

Prayer for Protection

Dear Heavenly Father,

I come before You, seeking Your protection and guidance. Keep me safe from harm and evil, and surround me with Your loving care.

As Your Word says in Psalm 91:4, **"He will cover you with his feathers, and under his wings you will find refuge; his faithfulness will be your shield and rampart."** (NIV).

I pray that You would be my refuge and fortress, my God in whom I trust. Protect me from the schemes of the enemy and keep me safe in Your loving arms.

Let Your protection be my comfort, hope, and strength. May I always find shelter in Your presence and peace in Your love.

In Jesus' name, I pray. Amen.

Prayer for Favor

Dear Heavenly Father,

I come before You, seeking Your favor and grace. Shine Your light upon me, and grant me Your blessing in all I do.

As Your Word says in Psalm 5:12, **"For you bless the righteous, O Lord; you cover them with your favor as with a shield." (ESV).**

I pray that You would grant me Your favor and that I may walk in Your blessing and grace. Let Your favor be my guide, comfort, and strength.

May Your favor open doors of opportunity, bring me wisdom and guidance, and surround me with Your loving care. Let Your favor be a shield of protection and a banner of hope in my life.

In Jesus' name, I pray. Amen.

CONCLUSION

Leah and Jake's story and reflections offer valuable insights into the importance of forgiveness, grace, and mercy in our relationships and spiritual lives. We learn that forgiveness is a process that can be difficult and may take time. Forgiveness requires effort and patience.

Grace and mercy are essential. It is crucial to extend grace and mercy to others, just as God extends them to us. This requires empathy, understanding, and a willingness to see beyond people's struggles and imperfections.

We see the power of prayer unraveling in Leah's marriage. Praying for others, even when they mistreat us, helps us develop a heart of love and forgiveness. It also acknowledges that people's behavior is ultimately between them and God.

Focusing on personal growth is key when dealing with a difficult situation. Instead of expecting others to change, we should focus on our own growth and transformation. This allows us to become better versions of ourselves and set a positive example for others. This also helps us to have a different perspective of our circumstances, allowing us to be the problem solver and not an addition to the problem.

Ultimately, God's love and treatment of us should inspire how we treat others. As mentioned, if God treated us the way we treat others, it would be a sobering reality check.

The question *"What if God treated you, the way you treated me?"* is a reminder that our actions have consequences, and we should strive to treat others with kindness and compassion. It encourages us to consider how God might perceive our behavior and attitudes toward others. Additionally:

- It's a call to empathy and understanding, to put ourselves in others' shoes and see things from their perspective.

- It reminds us that we are all children of God, deserving of love, respect, and kindness.

- It challenges us to examine our relationships and interactions with others, make amends, and change our ways to align with God's love and compassion.

- It's a powerful tool for personal growth and spiritual development, helping us to become more like God and to reflect His love and grace to others.

- It's a reminder that God's love and grace are not just for us but also for those around us and that we are called to extend that love and grace to others.

- It encourages us to practice forgiveness, mercy, and understanding, just as God has forgiven and shown mercy to us.

- It's a call to humility and self-reflection, recognizing our flaws and mistakes, and seeking to improve our relationships with others.

- It reminds us that our treatment of others is a reflection of our love for God and that we should strive to love and serve others as a way of worshiping and honoring Him.

As we conclude our journey through the transformative power of God's love, mercy, and forgiveness, may our lives reflect the divine grace bestowed upon us. Let us continue to embrace the liberating power of mercy, forgiveness, and love, shining as beacons of light for all to see.

May we carry the light of God's love in our hearts as we go forth, extending love and kindness to those around us. Let us remember that forgiveness is a continuous process of growth, healing, and transformation.

In the end, it is our surrender to God's love, mercy, and forgiveness that defines us. Resting in the assurance of our status as beloved children of God, may our lives serve as testimonies to the transformative power of His love to redeem and restore us.

ABOUT THE AUTHOR

Cheleta Buddo-Gayle is a devoted wife, mother, and multifaceted individual who excels as a writer, film and music producer, philanthropist, and entrepreneur. With a diverse range of talents and passions, she brings a unique perspective and creativity to all her endeavors. Yet, at the core of her being, Cheleta's heart  beats for ministry and serving the Lord with devotion. Her writing and creative endeavors are infused with a deep sense of purpose and faith, inspiring others to find their own path to spiritual fulfillment. Cheleta aims to uplift, empower, and bring hope to her audience through her work, reflecting her commitment to living a life of purpose and service.

Contact information

Christ RepresentHER
Cheleta Buddo-Gayle
Founder & CEO

@christrepresenther

christrepresenther@gmail.com

www.ingramcontent.com/pod-product-compliance
Lightning Source LLC
Chambersburg PA
CBHW042027050526
44107CB00103B/728